Advance Praise for Own Your Power

For years, I've witnessed Ginnette Baker crush it as a strong and successful businesswoman, a loyal and loving wife, a rock-star mom of two amazing kids, and a Godly woman of faith, and I've often wondered how she does it all. With *Own Your Power*, now I know, and she's sharing her power with the world so YOU can own yours; discover your "Why;" and like Ginnette, take hold of the life you were meant to live! *Own Your Power* is extremely well-written, is full of integrity and heart, is loaded with practical wisdom and application, and will motivate you in whatever stage of life you're in! A MUST-READ for all walks of life! I'm telling everyone I know!!

Les Norman
Former MLB Player, Jr. Olympic Gold Medalist, Radio Host, and Executive Leadership Consultant and Coach

"Own your power" is a quote I have heard a lot through the years. I do admit that until my forties, I never really embodied or understood what it means. Now, I understand it so much better, and this book has helped me understand myself and others so much more. Owning your power is a process that our mothers and other sheroes may not have been able to attain in their lifetimes, yet they wanted us to know this is possible in ours. I have had times in my past when I led with my ego and let my emotions take over. This is NOT owning my power. I refused to see the other party's viewpoint and immediately went into fight or flight mode.

After a childhood filled with abuse, abandonment, and rejection, I got used to doing things on my own, never asking for help. I thought I was owning my power. My actions led me to not relate well to others and see their stance as if it were always me against the world.

In my forties, wisdom started taking over. Owning your power is key and essential, yet it requires true commitment. Commitment to listening, to not seeing everyone as the enemy, and seeking to listen and understand and not just pop off a cutting response. It also requires loving myself and others as we all strive to survive and thrive in this crazy world!

Ginnette Baker, you have hit it out of the park with this book. You go deep and show how this process works. Like a muscle, you have to train your mind to know that every situation does not deserve your response. You cannot make sense of crazy, and we will all travel roads that will humble and mature us, opening doors, hearts, and minds.

Thank you, Ginnette! *Own Your Power* freaking rocks! Happy to support you and your message and own my power!

Precious L. Williams
The Pitch Queen and #KillerPitchMaster
CEO, Perfect Pitches by Precious

If you are ready to tap into your inner power and become the best version of yourself, then look no further than to the pages of this transformative book, *Own Your Power*! Ginnette's expert guidance has impacted countless individuals from young adults to seasoned professionals by challenging them to explore new ways of thinking and empowering them to achieve their goals.

As a contributing author in my book, *Heels to Deals: How Women are Dominating B2B Sales*, Ginnette's inspiring personal journey and story have been instrumental in helping others succeed. Her passion is unparalleled, and her dedication to empowering others in business is further evidenced by her role on my advisory board and as a mentor, focusing on closing the gender gap in B2B sales for my nonprofit, GirlzWhoSell. Trust me, Ginnette Baker's *Own Your Power* is a must-read for anyone looking to unleash their true potential.

Heidi Solomon-Orlick
Founder & CEO, GirlzWhoSell
Author, Keynote Speaker, and Podcast Host

Own Your Power is a must-read. Ginnette sheds profound light on ways to drive personal and professional success and takes you on a journey of self-discovery. She shares actionable and compelling "Power Points" followed by engaging stories to allow for contemplation and the ability to create needed next steps in life. I highly recommend reading *Own Your Power*!

Jennifer Ives
Founder, The JSI Group
Global Business Executive, Board Member,
Advisor, and Author

OWN
Your Power

OWN
Your Power

A Young Adult's Guide to Using Understanding, Confidence, Planning, Faith, and Adaptability to Get What You Want

GINNETTE BAKER

speaking·publishing·coaching
BMH
companies

BMcTALKS Press
4980 South Alma School Road
Suite 2-493
Chandler, Arizona 85248

Volume pricing is available to bulk orders placed by corporations, associations, and others. For bulk order details and for media inquiries, please contact BMcTALKS Press at info@bmtpress.com or 202.630.1218.

FIRST EDITION

Library of Congress Control Number: 2022922805

ISBN: 978-1-953315-25-0 (paperback)
ISBN: 978-1-953315-26-7 (eBook)

SELF-HELP / Communication and Social Skills
SELF-HELP / Personal Growth / Success

Interior design by Medlar Publishing Solutions Pvt Ltd., India.
Cover design by BMcTALKS Press

Printed in the United States of America.

Dedication

Thank you to the most amazing women in my life.

To my grandmother, I am thankful for every day you instilled in me the value to work hard for everything and that I can do anything I put my mind to no matter what obstacles I may face. I cannot wait for the day I get to hug you again.

To my mother, I am thankful for you showing me how to evaluate a situation and look for what is not always obvious to others. Thank you for teaching me to not be afraid, to ask for what I want, and to always trust my gut.

To my daughter, thank you for always believing in me. You have grown into an outstanding young lady with such a bright future. Thank you for pushing me to write this book and constantly pushing me to share my story.

I love you all.

Table of Contents

Introduction

Do not give away your power—take ownership of your thoughts, actions, and reactions that direct your life and everything you do.

Imagine being a child who was raised by a single mother who was raised by a single mother who was also raised by a single mother. That was my reality. When I was very young, starting at the age of three, my maternal grandmother would sit me at the dining room table and pretty much force me to complete worksheets, read books, and calculate math problems. When I was done and only when I was done, we would play cards—mostly solitaire—where I would help at first, then I began to play beside her with each of us playing our own games, racing to see who would finish placing all her cards in the correct order first. And on fun days, we would play gin rummy. But these games were not just for fun. As we played, we talked—mostly about life. And she imparted her many words of wisdom in only the way that a grandmother could. She told me over and over again "You will be strong, you will be confident, you can do anything a man can do, and you will be successful." From the time I was three years old and on, she wanted to instill this in my mind. And it worked!

Grandma was raised during a time when women struggled to achieve the same rights as men, and she had watched her own mother face these same challenges. When my grandmother's husband died unexpectedly of a heart attack in 1959, that left her all alone with three children—a sixteen-year-old, a ten-year-old, and a two-year-old—to provide for, but she was a strong woman who managed it with grace. However, due to laws at the time, she was limited as to where she could work and what she could do. She could not simply walk into any place of employment and think she could apply for the first position available, so she settled on being the school lunch lady; that positioned her to be with her girls and have some additional income.

It was not until 1973 that it became possible for women to apply for positions that had been previously reserved for men—higher-paying positions. This was the year that the Supreme Court upheld the 1968 Equal Employment Opportunity Commission ruling that sex-segregated help wanted ads were no longer permissible. And it was not until a year later in 1974 with the Equal Credit Opportunity Act that women could not be discredited based on their gender. But by then, her financial needs had shifted. These historic changes took place fourteen and fifteen years after her husband's death; they went into effect when two of her three girls were fully grown and able to fend for themselves, and the youngest was a teenager but only a year or two away from adulthood.

Being so abruptly subjected to this injustice at the time of her husband's death, she wanted to instill her words of power within me. She made sure to destroy any doubts that may have made me think that I did not have the same opportunities as anyone else no matter my gender or social status. It was up to me to earn my way and gain my results.

She passed away when I was almost twelve and didn't get to see me earn that way or gain those results, but I hear her words every day in my mind.

I stumbled along my path as I grew. I became pregnant at seventeen years old, and in an instant, all my hard work in school and dreams of college vanished. I was privileged enough to have an amazing family support group, but it wasn't until I woke up one day and, during a daily bible study devotional, I realized I was what was holding myself back.

While reading Acts 1:8 "But you will receive power when the Holy Spirit has come upon you, and you will be my witnesses …," it was like a slap in the face that awakened me. I was letting my circumstances and the small-minded views of what others felt was right or proper determine my future. I felt I had already thrown away a prosperous career because I was a young mom, no longer able to go to college and that it was important that I prove I was a good mom. I felt I could not ask for help or that I didn't deserve forgiveness for my past mistakes. I remembered, though, in that moment while reading that scripture, I was given God's grace and ultimately his power that made me see that I should allow my gifts to determine my potential. My grandmother's words rang in my ears once again, and in my mind I felt this message resonate—"Own your power!"

When I was in my twenties, I began repeating that mantra to myself—"Own your power! Stop giving your power away!" I would repeat these statements over and over in my mind while working full-time, being a wife and a mother, and attending school at night and on the weekends. I earned my bachelor's, graduating summa cum laude, and not too long after, I earned my master's in business. However, most of my learning occurred outside of the college classroom.

Inspired by amazing leaders I worked with, I wanted to gain their insight and knowledge at every turn—whether it was, in my spare time, reading books that they suggested, taking leadership assessments, or asking deeper questions to get their advice. I also quickly learned from bad leaders how *not* to act or how *not* to treat others. I felt God placed these individuals in my life—both the amazing leaders and those who weren't so amazing—to help direct my journey. And on this journey, even if I was not technically in a leadership position—I did not allow my official title to define my role in the company; anyone in any position can be a leader—so, I researched better alternatives when the "correct" leadership style wasn't readily apparent or clear to me.

Power Point

Anyone in any position can be a leader.

To reach others, I began using the same mantra—"Own your power! Stop giving your power away!"—For more than twenty years, I have fine-tuned this approach as a business leader in coaching my own employees, as a business mentor and coach to others, and in the classroom but from the other side of the desk as an educator. In 2010, I began to facilitate college courses at the bachelor's and master's levels. I wove these methodologies into the classroom, and they make their way into seminars and personal development engagements when I speak to young adults. I am constantly learning and sharing what has worked well for myself and for others with the goal of helping people who feel constricted by their circumstances (regardless of whether their situation is within their control or not). In short, I have made it a priority to mentor and help others in any way I can along their journey.

But what is your power? And how does a person give it away?

Your power is the strength of your thoughts, actions, and emotions. Giving it away is falling victim to the lies we tell ourselves, our unconscious biases, and our limiting beliefs. By placing fear before action, by not living to our full potential, and by not evolving and growing ourselves, we give away our power.

Power Point

Your power is the strength of your thoughts, actions, and emotions. Giving it away is falling victim to the lies we tell ourselves, our unconscious biases, and our limiting beliefs. By placing fear before action, by not living to our full potential, and by not evolving and growing ourselves, we give away our power.

Through many trials and tribulations, I started to document and outline lies, biases, and limiting beliefs in my own life, and I countered them with actions to take to overcome them. The answer—or the actions—was to own my power and to help those I mentor, educate, and coach to own their power so they can become the better version of themselves. Notice I did not write "best." That is because if we think we are living our "best" life, we can become complacent and do little to continue to improve and seek ways to grow. We need to seek to always work on how we become the better versions of who we were created to be in this life, and through these better versions, we can continue to grow.

I know I am nowhere close to what I see my full potential could be, and I am sure if you were honest, you would say the same.

Now, I can already hear naysayers.

"I *am* the best version of me!"

"God made me perfect the way I am!"

"I am who I am."

Notice each of those statements includes "I am." If you are always focused on who or what you are in the present moment, you do not become who you are supposed to be in this world. When you own your power, you make an effort every day to achieve your full potential while impacting this world no matter how big or small—for me that revolves around my Christian beliefs in Jesus Christ.

Power Point

If you are always focused on who or what you are in the present moment, you do not become who you are supposed to be in this world.

As you read *Own Your Power*, you will quickly learn that I rely on my strong Christian faith. For me, my power comes from the Holy Spirit and my discernment for God's will for my life. And every time I give away my power, I diminish my greater purpose and what God has as my full potential in this life. For you, your greater purpose could be something else, or maybe you are still trying to figure what is your greater purpose.

In 2016, I recall sitting with a friend one day when she voiced, out of frustration, "I feel like I should be doing something bigger with my life." As I sat there, I reflected on her comment, and silently told myself "Nope. I do not feel that way." I feel like I am doing what I am called to do; however, flashforward three years to 2019, and I felt God lay on my heart something different; and a different calling or purpose began to take seed in my heart. So, it is okay if you are not sure in this moment or if you feel like you might know but aren't 100% certain. If you do not know, as you read *Own Your Power*, reflect on what that could be for you, and open your heart.

When you understand your motivations, concerns, and reactions in challenging situations, you will know what areas hold you back from evolving as a person.

The first step is to become honestly aware of the pitfalls that make you stumble or that cause you to go down a victim's path.

The second step is to turn around your perspective to abandon the thoughts of being a victim and to find the source of your power that will propel you in new directions you never imagined.

This sets you up to evolve and reach your full potential. It would be a shame to the rest of the world if we never got to see your full potential and the impact you could make. We were each created to serve a purpose. Start to explore yours as you read each chapter, paying close attention to chapter 3 where more specific techniques are covered, but each chapter guides you in discerning this for yourself.

In *My Utmost for His Highest*, Oswald Chambers writes "God did not direct His call to Isaiah—Isaiah overheard God saying, '… who will go for Us?' The call of God is not for a select few but for everyone. Whether I hear God's call or not depends on the condition of my ears, and exactly what I hear depends upon my spiritual attitude." So, while it may feel uncomfortable to do so, still hear and accept the call, then identify your purpose.

It was nowhere near my comfort zone to share in book format the ideas that I have developed over the years on how to own your power and not give it away. Writing this book pushed me to open up old wounds, share uncomfortable concepts, and face the possibility of criticism. But ultimately, through pressure from my daughter to act on what I felt I was called to do, I took a leap of faith and continued to press forward in owning my own power with the goal of helping others.

So, congratulations to you! Just by picking up this book, you are taking a step forward to own your power and no longer give it away. Each chapter of this book is designed to dive deeply into exactly how you can begin to do just that. The chapters are as follows:

- **The Power in Understanding**
- **The Power in Confidence**
- **The Power in Planning**
- **The Power in Faith**
- **The Power in Adaptability**

I provide detailed situations and stories that illustrate the actions to take, but do not limit yourself to what is between the two covers of this book. We are each beautifully and uniquely made, and these examples and anecdotes are here as starting points for you to think of your own circumstances and help you identify how you can personally stop giving away your power. I encourage you to be honest with yourself. Journal as you read, and create steps to put in place to immediately to start owning your power at home, work, and school; with your friends; and in your financial wellbeing. This focus and insight will result in your communications improving; you will know why and how to respond differently. It will help you overcome what is holding you back from setting new goals; how to execute a plan of action to achieve those goals even when obstacles arise; and finally, how to be adaptable in finding a new path or a new way of thinking differently when dealing with difficult people or situations.

Finally, once you own your power, you explore how to find your superpower in a bonus section. This section covers how you move forward with your True North, developing your personal brand. Having a personal brand is what will guide you and direct you. This brand will be your constant reminder of what you want for your life and career—what you want to project and become. When you focus on it, it will help guide your decisions and hold you personally accountable. It will also help you determine whether the advice you seek from external sources applies to you, whether the advice will work, or if you should simply disregard it.

We cannot be great at everything, but there are some things that are truly natural to us; the bonus section leads you to find yours, to find your superpower and leverage your superpower for good. As for everything else, we can work towards and begin to learn more about ourselves in the process.

I hope you are excited to begin this journey to own your power!

CHAPTER 1

The Power in Understanding

"When you say 'I' and 'my' too much, you lose the capacity to understand the 'we' and 'our.'"

—Steve Maraboli, American speaker, author, athlete, and veteran

You Can't Teach Me Anything I Don't Already Know

In 2010, I began teaching part-time at a local university where my power of understanding was put to the test in the very first class. It was an undergraduate business communication course that met at night to accommodate full-time working adults who had returned to school to earn their degrees. These students were my passion. I understood their perspectives because I had done the same—worked a full-time job while raising kids full-time and going to college full-time.

The classes were always very small and intimate with only seven to ten students, which worked well because it made it easier for me to make a conscious effort to get to know everyone and to do what I really enjoyed—getting to not only facilitate the class but also mentor students.

When I walked in the first day, I was pretty energetic! On this first day, though, Dante did not particularly care for my enthusiasm. To get to know everyone, I went around the classroom and asked each student to tell me their name, what their job was during the day, goals or hopes for this class, and their goals once they received their degree. In each class, I wrote down exactly what each person said so when I gave feedback on their assignments, I was able to personalize my comments. Some students were very generic while others shared their life stories. Either way, I did my very best to provide helpful and individualized feedback based on what I learned about each student in class.

But Dante stopped me in my tracks that day.

We went around the room with a relatively smooth flow until it was Dante's turn. He boldly stated "My name is Dante, and I am here to get this stupid piece of paper that is holding me back from a promotion I deserve. And no offense, I know you will be upset by this as most of you professors are, but by the looks of it, I doubt you can teach me anything that I do not already know. Every class seems to be a waste of time."

He had a smirk on his face as the words left his mouth. I could tell he adamantly *felt* what he was saying, and I sensed that the chip he carried on his shoulder was well deserved from a hard life he had lived. My response to Dante could have gone in several directions. I was the hired facilitator of the course, and that is a position that automatically came with a line of respect; but as you looked at the other faces in the room, you could tell the collective thought was he might have crossed that line.

Do I establish my authority? Do I just ignore the moment? What would be the best next steps? As he spoke, I did my best to remain calm, to not take his words personally, and to evaluate and understand the situation.

I come from the viewpoint of positive intent. This assumption is that 99% of people go through life everyday wanting to do good, to better themselves, and be a positive force in the world. But, sometimes, somewhere along the way, something happens, and we get distracted. No one truly wants to be a jerk, but it might come across that way. Because of this, I try to look at the positive intent in every situation. Therefore, I began to evaluate the situation with Dante, silently putting forth an honest effort to understand his viewpoint and where he was coming from.

I calculated that we were about the same age, however, I always seem to appear younger than I am, so he might have assumed that I had no real-world experience and had only college knowledge. He was an African American male; I was a Caucasian female. One could have surmised from these quick observations, with seemingly nothing in common, there was nothing to learn from each other. And in that swift assessment, I felt compassion and identified his positive intent.

I quickly replied with "I see you are a bold communicator, and I love that! Being open and honest is a terrific way to be a leader. I look forward to learning from each other in this class." And then I went on to cover the first lesson.

By choosing not to be angry or to not let my ego get in the way and by being willing to meet him where he was in his thinking at that moment, I did not give away my power. Had I matched his energy, I would have given away my power. Had I directly responded to what seemed like disrespect to my position and my authority, then I would have given away my power. My assessment and my choices in that moment helped me own my power; my choices showed him respect—respect that, at the time, he felt he didn't have—and that I was strong enough to meet him where he was so we could achieve success together.

Taking ownership of your thoughts, actions, and reactions in everything you do is the first step to owning your power. Too often people get so caught up in their own story or their own dialogue that they do not consider another's point of view. Mentally stepping back and looking at the situation as well as the person's perspective, background, and beliefs, then trying to find common ground is hard to do but is so worth it in the long run.

It is only natural to impose your personal background and history onto a situation. In fact, it is our previous experiences that help train our brains as children to grow and to anticipate how to react and how we bring context into new situations. But, it is also what can lead to an unconscious bias and, thus, prevent us from meeting new people, or it can cause fear to restrict us from embracing new situations. And in that fear, we often make assumptions and, consequently, give away our power.

Over the eight weeks of class with Dante, that chip he had on his shoulder the first day shrank or altogether disappeared. He ended up being *overly* engaged in class, willing to share his work situations, looking for advice, as well as sharing advice! We challenged the thoughts of everyone in the classroom and created innovative solutions together, teaching lessons of working as a team. After he completed my class, he went on to earn his degree, and I continued to follow him on LinkedIn to watch the evolution of his career. I often reflect on how proud I am of his accomplishments. I also often reflect on how miserable I would have been facilitating that class if that first day had gone differently. And it might have if I had not learned at a very young age to seek to first understand and not to let my arrogance and temper get in the way.

But we're all human, and not losing your temper is definitely an art versus a science. I am extremely hot-tempered, and you can tell by the look on my face exactly how I feel about a person or a situation. My facial expressions can evoke a whole different language; I have to make a concerted effort to control them every day—and I often fail! My mother was a smart woman who knew my highly competitive spirit would be the driving force behind me finding any way to win in any situation. She noticed my hot temper at a young age and would always tell me "You lose your temper, you lose the argument." Not only did she inspire and teach me with her words, but she also lived by and followed her own lessons even when it would have been much easier to do the opposite.

Power Point

You lose your temper, you lose the argument.

Remember, you don't have to go toe-to-toe. You don't have to always match wits. You don't have to let your temper get the better of you. You have to ask yourself what you want the outcome to be, if you will be owning your power in the process, then what actions will get you that outcome and will allow you to always own your power.

The Help You Ask For Is Less About You and Is More the Person Who Helps You

Being a single mom in a southern Baptist church is a hard job.

Even after my mom got married to a man who had no children and who had never been married before, life was not much easier for her. It was viewed as a disgrace that my mother made the decision to stand up from a physically abusive marriage with her first husband to find a better life for her children and herself. The church would not even allow her new husband to be an usher because he had married a divorced woman. It mattered not that she stood by the grace of God and still faithfully attended church to make sure her children knew God and that they were blessed by His grace and mercy.

Some would have judged her again and said that this church was not an environment she should have stayed in, but she was faithful in God's Word and forgiveness and did not worry about the judgement of men. And through this, I saw that, as other women in the church would slight her, she just smiled her beautiful smile and calmly continued. Oh, how I wish to have the grace she portrayed and her strength to engage in forgiveness with what appeared to be little to no effort on her part.

The power of understanding my mother's actions was hard at the time, and it was not until years later, being a mother myself, did I fully grasp her sacrifice and strength in choosing the path she felt was best and to not let the adversity she faced derail her. This happened quite a bit growing up where I never understood why she did what she did. I think we all tend to question or criticize how someone can choose a path when an obvious easier choice is right in front of them. However, the truth is it is a critical error to judge someone who is facing obstacles and life circumstances that are completely different from what you are facing or that are obstacles and circumstances you cannot even begin to imagine. Saying "Oh, I would never do that" is such an easy assertion when you do not have the full story or the complete picture. And even if you have faced a similar situation, details, actions, and consequences are sure to be entirely different. In actuality, you cannot be absolutely certain of the decisions you will make if forced to do so. Judging someone for the choice they make instead of seeking to understand their perspective is what holds us back from owning our power.

Power Point

It's a critical error to judge someone who is facing obstacles and life circumstances that you cannot even begin to imagine.

I remember how our church would host the most elaborate Christmas pageants where literally busloads of people would come from all over the Midwest to be in the audience. The event took place over the course of two full weekends and required so much planning and preparation over the year. My mom was working on costumes—if my memory serves me correctly—and she has a flawless sense of color and understanding of color pallets. However, she specifically went over to a lady who was quite prominent in the "inner circle,"—a queen bee of sorts … I am sure you know the type—and asked the lady if she would help her select the perfect material for our costumes. Now, with a large group of people around with all eyes on her, the woman had no choice but to agree to assist—it was the Christian thing to do, right?—and in fact, she looked quite happy to share her exquisite knowledge in all things pageant. But given how she'd treated my mom in the past, without an audience, she likely would have given a much different response.

Later that night, I asked my mom why she asked for Queen Bee's help when, in fact, she could have picked as good of if not better materials for the costumes. She looked at me and gently told me that sometimes when we ask for help, we do it to help others rather than to help ourselves. At the time, I could not understand this lesson. It made no sense to me. This woman was not nice to my mother. I saw it firsthand as I was friends with her daughter; we spent time together all the time, and I saw their interactions were strained. Why would my mother admit even more weakness to a woman who already looked down on her?

It would be years later when I would understand and fully learn the lesson my mom was trying to teach me.

It was prior to my mother remarrying, and I was playing at that friend's house. When my mother came to pick me up, Queen Bee was very blunt with her and said "You give our husbands a bad idea. You let them think we can do this on our own," alluding to my mother's seemingly effortless movement through life as a single parent. I am not sure how my mother responded to the situation, but I do know that instead of taking this woman's quite pointed comment in a hateful way, she embraced the comment so she could understand the woman's fear. My mom realized that this woman saw her strength and that could have felt intimidating, or the woman may have even been fearful of my mom's show of strength, evoking a weakness in herself. My mom was never angry for how the woman made her feel and had the power of understanding and showed compassion in her actions in that moment. This was something she already sensed, and for that reason, she asked for her costume help years before. She understood that this woman had the desire to feel needed and important, and if my mom could help her in that endeavor, then she would. A true lesson in owning your own power is understanding the importance of putting kindness and the thoughts of others first. This is a lesson that I would try to duplicate and incorporate into my life thereafter.

———————————————————✸

Power Point

A true lesson in owning your own power: Put kindness and the thoughts of others first.

✸———————————————————

Too often, being nice or the act of kindness is seen as a weakness. The conventional thought is men are supposed to be strong and masculine, and that strength and masculinity are often viewed as the opposite of what it means to be kind. Following that line of thinking, oftentimes, women are expected to downplay their kindness to not appear weak in front of others—or to appear strong. I was once criticized by a female peer business executive who, in a passive aggressive jab, said she would rather die than be called nice or kind after someone complimented me for my kindness. However, being kind is a sign of strength.

According to Charlotte Armitage, a media and business psychologist, "To truly offer kindness shows a level of psychological strength and resilience which is grounded in acceptance of oneself. This level of acceptance requires a significant amount of internal strength and takes hard work to achieve." Showing kindness is a form of respect, and it's a form of strength. No matter someone's identity, race, or station in life, anyone and everyone can be shown a form of kindness. And in doing so, you own your power of understanding.

Power Point

Showing kindness is not a weakness. It's a form of respect, and it's a form of strength.

A Lion Does Not Concern Itself With a Sheep

In today's age of social media, we often find ourselves seemingly unable to control our emotions and lean into understanding others when faced with what feels like a need to "clap back"—to correct a wrong and publish "the correction" for the world to see. This desire to protect our reputation or the feelings of our friends or family members coupled with the ability to respond in seconds at the stroke of a button and the tap of a fingertip becomes a compelling situation. On social media, finding understanding is difficult as we often cannot decipher someone's true intent or understand why they felt comfortable to air their feelings so broadly for the world to see.

Once, while having coffee with a friend, she shared a situation wherein she did not own her power. It was one where she fell into a trap that she regretted—the simple action of firing back on social media when she felt she and her family were being attacked in a post by an acquaintance. Of course, the situation was vague, but all parties involved knew what it was about while hundreds of others had no clue; but everyone seemed to tune in to watch the social media showdown.

"Why did I do that?" she asked, shaking her head in frustration. She continued by pointing out "I literally played right into her hand. I am better than that!" Hindsight is always 20/20, right? And in this moment, she realized she had given away her power.

In the busy coffee shop, as I looked across the table, I realized that anyone can fall victim to this desire to immediately respond. If this well-educated, accomplished female business executive struggled with this overwhelming desire to correct the social media cycle of misconception being displayed, then how could *any* of us overcome it? Some may think what she did was fine and justified. But at the end of the day, did her actions change anything? Did it somehow make the other person understand her point of view? And for the people on the outside of the situation looking in, reading that post, did it cast any one of those ladies in a positive light? If we are honest, the answer is NO!

But when faced with the temptation to fire back on social media or elsewhere, remember "A lion never loses sleep over the opinions of sheep." If you are a lion, you are powerful and in control, and you clearly understand that sheep do not pose a threat to you in any way. They are weaker in fortitude, standing, and mentality. Therefore, in that understanding, you do not care about their opinions.

Power Point

A lion never loses sleep over the opinions of sheep.

This was the case with my friend, and it was the reason she regretted her actions so much. It took her down to a lower level and on such a public platform, and in the end, it changed nothing.

However, she learned a lesson—to use her power of understanding going forward to think and assess before reacting and to own her power.

Listen to Understand, Not to Respond

Have you ever witnessed two people arguing, but when you sit back and listen or read the comments, they are arguing the same point?

I laugh because I see it happening in my own home all the time. One night, when my son was home visiting from college, he walked into my bedroom and said, "Do you hear them downstairs?" He was referring to my husband and daughter who were having an elevated conversation, to be kind. Now, I love my husband and my daughter dearly, but their stubbornness is identical and sometimes comical. My son exclaimed, "Do they even realize they are arguing the same point?!" My response was simple. "No, they do not, but they will figure it out soon. And then both will not admit it. Welcome to my life." He looked a little annoyed that I was laughing about it, but in all honesty, at that point, there was nothing I could do.

Later, I had a conversation with my daughter about how to listen to understand and how to communicate by owning her power of understanding. I told her paying attention to context clues was important. Truly listen to his words without automatically thinking about how to respond. Because when you "listen" while simultaneously crafting your response, you're not even listening at all. With her tone, she automatically goes on the defense and doesn't listen to one word. I advised she consider closing her eyes to force herself to actively and carefully listen. Ask questions to understand him more; doing so could have helped them realize they were actually in agreement the whole time but were simply using different terms.

That was not the first conversation nor was it the last we have had on this subject, but as a young woman, I wanted her to quickly realize how she gave away her power by not listening to understand because, unfortunately, women are often viewed as more emotional or irrational than men, therefore, discrediting our ideas. Whether this is true or not, it doesn't matter; the goal is to be aware of this bias, so we have to work harder to overcome this perception. And using the power of understanding is the way to achieve it faster. To own your power, listen first to understand, not to respond.

Power Takeaways

The power of understanding is broad. It's the power of understanding a person's perspectives, understanding a person's motives, understanding a situation, and listening to clearly understand the words being said.

- Assess the positive intent of others, and show kindness in your approach is a way to own your power.
- When you let your temper do the work for you or when you make assumptions that are not based on facts, it's a fast way to give away your power. Choose to operate in fact and to not let your temper lead the way.
- Understand how your actions and reactions impact how you can make a difference and using that understanding to own your power is imperative.
- Listen with the intent to understand words without emotions and not to just respond or react in a manner that would ultimately give your power away.
- Owning your power of understanding is meeting others where they are while understanding your own actions and reactions and how they impact a situation.

Power Thinking and Journaling

- Are you giving away your power of understanding? How can you tell?
- How can you change the way you seek to understand?
- What techniques can help you improve in these areas?

_____

_____

_____

_____

_____

_____

_____

_____

Books to Help You Own
Your Power of Understanding

Understanding Other People: The Five Secrets to Human Behavior by Beverly D. Flaxington

Personality Plus: How to Understand Others by Understanding Yourself by Florence Littauer

How to Read People Like a Book: A Guide to Speed-Reading People, Understand Body Language and Emotions, Decode Intentions, and Connect Effortlessly by James W. Williams

CHAPTER 2

The Power
in Confidence

"If you have no confidence in self, you are twice defeated in the race of life. With confidence, you have won even before you have started."

—Cicero, Roman statesman, lawyer, scholar,
philosopher, and academic skeptic

Is it Nature or Nurture?

Do you know someone who always appears naturally confident? They exude confidence even as they walk into a room with their shoulders back and their head held high. They speak with authority and do not waiver in the face of opposition. Do you know someone like that? I know I do, and I have analyzed if this is nature (they were naturally born with it) or if it's nurture (something they have to work on.)

And whether a person is born with confidence or had to work on it, each person presents her/himself as of one of three types of confident people. One type of confidence is that of a person who has the ability to not worry about what others think of them. Recall the lion's lack of concern over the sheep's perception of the lion in Chapter 1: The Power in Understanding. These people really understand that there are very few people who have influence over our lives. They know there are people in our lives forever, for a season, and for a moment. We need to truly understand and decide if these are people who we care about what they think. Either by the way someone is raised from childhood or if there is a natural attribute that makes this approach easier for some, this is an area that anyone can begin to realize, immediately evaluate, and own whether they will allow it to impact them.

Power Point

There are people in our lives forever, for a season, and for a moment.

The second type of confident people are what I call the crazies and the crooks. This is an area that is important to understand so we do not fall into this trap ourselves and so we can identify it when we see this happening in the world.

According to the late philosopher and essayist Bertrand Russell, "The whole problem with the world is that fools and fanatics are always so certain of themselves, but wiser people are so full of doubts." This idea is portrayed in a psychological model, the Dunning-Kruger Effect.

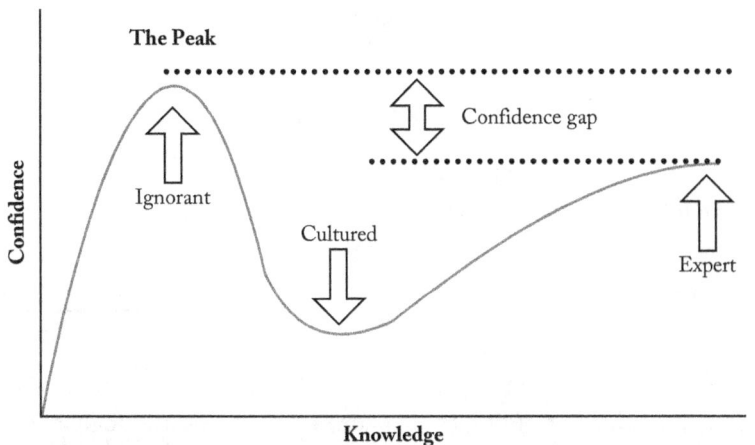

Dunning-Kruger Effect

In simple terms, the Dunning-Kruger Effect measures someone's confidence in comparison to their knowledge. When we first learn something, we have a higher confidence level and overestimate our overall knowledge. But as our knowledge increases, we realize we know less than we thought we did, and our confidence goes down. When we keep learning, our knowledge increases, and even at expert levels, we now have the knowledge that things are constantly evolving and changing so our confidence levels out as well.

So, those people who seem to know everything all the time or those fanatics who seem to have only one side of the story and are not open to seeing others' points of view may appear confident, but that is not the confidence that will, at the end of the day, bring about owning your power to improve your life. This is more ego than confidence. Ego is stating "I am better than you" while confidence is stating "I work every day to be the better version of me."

Power Point

Ego is stating "I am better than you" while confidence is stating "I work every day to be the better version of me."

And finally, the third type of confident person is one who identifies what is holding them back and continuously focuses on overcoming their obstacles. Remember this: You do not decide your future. You decide your habits, and your habits decide your future. If none of the confidence types seem to align with you, the good news is the power of confidence develops over time—it's something you work on every day.

Power Point

You do not decide your future. You decide your habits, and your habits decide your future.

Address the Fear, the Shame, and the Lies You Tell Yourself

"I wish I had your confidence in everything."

That's what a coworker said to me out of the blue while on a business trip, having dinner, and engaging in a casual conversation. I was taken aback by the comment. Confidence is something I felt like I was constantly working on. I have always been outspoken, asking questions, and unafraid to point out ideas or make suggestions in the work setting. I was even once told I could make a cup of coffee nervous, which I took as a compliment. However, I never viewed myself as confident.

In fact, I was constantly focused on trying to be *more* confident. To figure out what it was my coworker was seeing, I started to take stock of all the actions I had taken to improve my confidence—articles or books I had read, speakers I had listened to, leaders I tried to learn best practices from—and as I sat back and thought, it hit me. I began portraying confidence by focusing on what was holding me *back* in those areas. And there were three important areas that I worked on every day—three areas that I *still* work on—in order to own my power of confidence. The first is addressing fear; the second is facing shame I felt; and finally, the third is not believing lies I once told myself. And I want you to do the same.

Is the Fear Real or Imagined?

Before you can address something, you have to clearly understand what it is, and to address fear, you must first define it. Fear is a reaction that arises from the threat of harm—either physical, emotional, or psychological—real or imagined.

Wow! "Real or imagined"—what are we making up in our minds versus what is in actuality happening around us? This reminds me of a colleague who often asks "Is that the reality of the situation, or is that the story you told yourself?" Let that sit with you for a moment.

To be honest, most of the time, I have a full-blown two-act musical with fully choreographed sections going on in my mind before I realize that is not *even* the reality of the situation! I have imposed my own ideas, my own fears, and my own beliefs onto the situation instead of taking the situation for what is, springing into action, and facing my perceived fear. What are we afraid of, though? What stops us? Is it what others may say, what others may think, or whether others won't like us anymore? But remember to ask yourself who are these "others," and should you care? Take a hard look at why you are giving away your power to others.

Power Point

Remember to ask yourself who are these "others," and should you care?

A young lady by the name of Sara overheard a conversation I was having with a friend in a public place. After the conversation finished, I sat alone, but Sara came over, apologized for interrupting me and for eavesdropping on my conversation, and introduced herself. From what she heard, she felt I gave really good business advice. As such, she wanted to know if she could run a business idea by me. I was pleasantly surprised by her confidence to just come up to me, but I had the time and felt it was definitely worth it to listen and assist to the best of my ability. I spent the next thirty minutes chatting with Sara about her business problem and ideas to solve it.

Sara went into great detail about her current work environment, revealing the main reason she approached me was because she had shared her idea with a colleague and, basically, had been given all the reasons (personally and business-wise) why it wouldn't work. And therefore, she had decided to put it to the side and not focus on it. But, in overhearing my conversation with my friend, she realized it *was* a good idea, and she wanted to do it.

I know I have been in that situation—where I have been excited about an idea or an opportunity; but someone, in so many terms, popped my balloon, and I was no longer excited. This is exactly what had happened to Sara. I asked her if any of those points from her colleague had validity. But before she could answer, I continued that if they had validity, then that is awesome because now she has a list of obstacles she can figure out how to overcome, to further build upon her business concept. And if some of the reasons Sara's colleague listed are not valid concerns, then she just takes them as someone else's personal opinion, but that opinion shouldn't deter her. Sara had a long journey ahead to fully build out the concept, but in that brief conversation, it was like a lightbulb went off. She realized she gave up too soon, that she took the *one* colleague's feedback as a sure sign that her business idea would lead to nothing but failure, and completely gave away her power.

In our society, where every aspect of our life seems to get broadcasted on social media, this fear is more apparent than ever. What if I cannot post that idea as a success? What if I can't say that I won? Or worse, what if I cannot post that my child is the best?

If a parent would rather see their children win a trophy at a lower level than push them to face adversity and challenge them to excel and compete at the highest level possible, then they are establishing a different (and possibly questionable) precedent for their child. This child, then, will feel like if they are not always winning, then they are failing, and honestly, in life, we fail a lot more than we win; but that is how we grow. Now, that might exaggerate the situation to an extreme, but ask anyone involved in childhood sports or activities of any kind which is a reality that our children are facing in this social-media-first world.

Power Point

In life, we fail a lot more than we win, but that is how we grow.

Failure is in the moment and a fleeting moment at that, so learn from it and continue to push forward. Famous artist and poet Michelangelo wrote "The greater danger for most of us is not that our aim is too high and we miss it but that it is too low and we reach it." What fear is holding you back from aiming high?

Power Point

What fear is holding you back from aiming high?

Assign Shame to Conscious Choices, Not Uncontrollable Circumstances

So much shame exists … Shame in how we look, how we talk, our social status, where we grew up, our education, poor choices in the past, the consequences of those choices—while unjustified, such shame can be quite common.

And that was the second area that was holding back my confidence. I lacked confidence because of feelings of shame from not only decisions I had made in my past but also shame from what I had no control over of but shame that I felt nonetheless. But American author Ann Patchett had it right with this quote: "Shame should be reserved for the things we choose to do. Not the circumstances that life puts on us."

Power Point

"Shame should be reserved for the things we choose to do. Not the circumstances that life puts on us." —Ann Patchett, American author

---

My daughter was diagnosed with a learning disability at age seven. She was pulled out of the mainstream classroom to begin learning different techniques and tools to help her learn in a way that was a better fit for her. Although she has an extremely high IQ, she simply learns differently than 90% of the population, and we were blessed with the assistance of some amazing educators to help her. The way her brain processes concepts differently—which honestly makes her abilities in mathematics and the arts more powerful—held her back in other areas such as reading and writing. With each passing year, she learned better tips and tricks that would help her operate in a traditional classroom, but even with the tips and tricks, she still needed accommodations in the classroom.

She soon realized she was different, and this difference created shame. She felt something was wrong with her, and as a result, she did not want others to know and would do anything to avoid others finding out.

When she was in high school, she even refused to engage in game night with a friend's family because she did not want them to discover she was different. It took a while, but she recognized that the way her brain works is actually really beautiful, and it gives her amazing creative abilities that we have coined as her "superpower." For years, she let that shame control her, and she has to make an effort every day to not fall back into that trap.

Now that she recognizes this shame, she has changed the narrative of her personal dialogue, that this is a blessing, and nothing should hold back her confidence. Her mantra is "My story is what made me … I was born with a purpose, and my job in the world is to live out that purpose. And if I don't do that, *that* is what is shameful."

Power Point

Your story is what made you. You were born with a purpose, and your job in the world is to live out that purpose. And if you don't do that, *that* is what is shameful.

But she did not arrive at this root cause overnight and definitely not at the age of seven. Getting to the root cause of what is holding you back from being confident is powerful, and it takes time. To do this work, a technique I like to use is the "Five Whys."

This technique was an original concept developed by Japanese inventor and founder of Toyota Industries Corporation Sakichi Toyoda. He stated that "by repeating 'why' five times, the nature of the problem as well as its solution becomes clear." Although this concept was originally developed for business issues and process mapping, when I first learned this concept in business, I quickly realized it could be applied to any and every problem or concept including personal lives. So, when asking yourself what is holding you back from being confident, ask yourself "why" until you get to the true root cause. This will require you to be very honest with yourself and face past situations you have often tried to avoid or deflect. However, that root cause can usually fall into one of three categories: fear, shame, or the lies we tell ourselves.

A great example of asking yourself "why" to get at the true root cause is a passage in American actress and producer Viola Davis's memoir *Finding Me*. This questioning takes place when her high school science teacher gave her a pamphlet about a national arts and talent search competition and thought she should apply, entering in the drama category. She later discussed the opportunity with her Upward Bound counselor, Jeff, coming up with every reason in the book to *not* complete the application, an application that required a video submission of herself performing two monologues.

Her initial reaction was "But I can't do it."

Jeff looked at the pamphlet then asked, "Why can't you do it?"

For every excuse she came up with *not* to apply, he met it with a response that included an unspoken "why" query.

She told him she didn't have a VHS tape to make the recording.

He volunteered to get a tape for her. *(Now, why can't you do it?)*

Then she said she didn't have the $15 application fee.

He said he'd get her a waiver. *(Now, why can't you do it?)*

Then she said she didn't have anywhere to record video of herself performing the requisite monologues.

He told her he could get her in at the TV station on the campus of Rhode Island College to take care of the recordings. *(Now, why can't you do it?)*

Finally out of excuses and no more responses to why she couldn't apply to the talent search competition, it all boiled down to this one statement she eventually writes: "I didn't believe I had a chance." But she did, and—spoiler alert—she was accepted into the program that included an all-expenses paid trip to Miami!

Again, that root cause of shame is identified by asking why over and over again.

And what if the shame is a result of something that is in your control? Maybe it is the hidden guilt of past mistakes that makes you feel as if you aren't deserving of a situation, therefore, you give away your power and, consequently, hold yourself back. Sometimes your worst enemy is your own memory, so how do you let it go and forgive yourself in order to feel worthy?

Power Point

Sometimes your worst enemy is your own memory.

Getting pregnant at seventeen years old, changing the entire course of my life, was an event I continuously felt shameful for throughout my career and my personal life. Even though my son was a complete blessing and I actually could never imagine my life any better than how it is, I felt undeserving of how I came to be in certain situations because I chose a non-traditional educational path in order to be a mom first and foremost. I never shared my age with anyone, and to hide my shame, I just let them assume I was much older than I was. While working full-time and being a mom full-time, I also attended school, first, a local community college, then a local state university. It took me a little longer than most, trying to juggle it all, but I got it done.

Shortly after I earned my bachelor's degree, I interviewed for a promotion. My company had just gone through a merger, and there was a mix of senior level leaders who were all learning how to work and partner together. I had an interview with one of these new leaders from the acquired company, having come highly recommended for the job from my current leadership team. Always eager to learn, I was excited for the interview and to meet someone from the new company. Not so fast with the excitement, though.

At the beginning of the interview, the interviewer's first comment was a scoff at my degree and from where I received it. He was fortunate enough to have attended a high-profile east coast school that had a leading business degree program, which he proudly touted. I had, however, earned a liberal arts degree from a local hometown university. Within an instant, I lost all confidence I had going into the interview, and I felt shame. I forgot about all my hard work of raising a family, working full-time while attending school full-time, and graduating summa cum laude with my bachelor's. I was immediately mentally transported to reminders of not getting the traditional education with a true business degree.

Needless to say, I didn't get that promotion. However, after I realized how weak I felt in letting my shame control me and giving away my power, I thought of my grandmother and her influential words to me. I took action, and I took my power back. Within a couple of weeks, I was sitting for the Graduate Management Admission Test (GMAT) and applying to MBA programs, which I completed a few years later. I had to learn that my choices were *my* choices, that they created the person I am now, and that is not something to feel shame about. Feeling confident in the person I am now is what I use to own my power.

Don't Believe a Lie

"I could never do that."

"I am not smart enough."

"I'm too thin, too thick, too old, too young, too _____."

(Fill in the blank with your own limiting belief you tell yourself.)

In 2019, *Psychology Today* reported that by age seventeen, 78% of girls are unhappy with their bodies, and more than 90% admit to feeling pressure to look a certain way or would change something about how they look if they could. For girls with low self-esteem, 75% of them reported engaging in negative activities such as cutting, bullying, smoking, drinking, or disordered eating.

Our own internal dialogue creates an entire story based on the perception of how we view ourselves whether the story is filled with truth or lies. Gaining your confidence is done by unpacking what those limiting beliefs are that you constantly tell yourself. The next time you tell yourself a limiting belief, turn it around.

Instead of "I can't do that," what if you *could* do that? What small step can you take today that will get you closer to being able to do that? What resources do you have at your disposal that will help you?

Instead of thinking you're not smart enough, why do you feel that you are not smart enough, and what action can you take (engage in self-study; enroll in school; read a book, listen to a podcast, or get coaching to address a deficit you have) to change that?

Instead of "I never get what I want," or "I'm too this, too that, or too 'something else,'" what do you need to do to help you be able to go after what you want? What do you need to do to change or to get past what you think is to "too X" about yourself?

My first job out of high school was a position at a local credit union where I was given the opportunity to conduct teen financial fitness classes. The goal of these classes or seminars was to help break the cycle of poor financial decisions. When I left the credit union to take a new job, a co-op electric company contacted me, informing me that one of their board members had seen me at a credit union conducting the seminar, and they wanted to ask me about facilitating the financial fitness class for a group of teens graduating high school who had each been awarded a college scholarship through a fund sponsored by the community. I had just left the credit union, so I let them know that, thinking with me no longer being in the credit union's employ, they would not want me. But they pushed on, indicating they would compensate me for my time and my travel, which was approximately a two-hour drive. I was excited and said "yes!"

That led to me developing a two-hour workshop on goal setting and financial awareness planning for teens and young adults. Two weeks later, I received a call from another institution that was on the other side of the state, approximately four hours away, asking for the same engagement! I was blown away, but this time I said "no." I was only twenty-one years old at the time, and I had just found out I was pregnant with my second child. My husband worked more than forty hours a week and remember—I had just started a new job. But none of that was the real reason I declined the offer.

The real reason was because I did not know my own value. I felt shameful, and I felt imposter syndrome as I did not have my degree yet. I was working on it, but I was far from done. I told myself lies—"they must have misunderstood, they really do not want me, they don't know who I am because I am nobody, they want someone qualified, and I am NOT qualified." And that led to my fear—fear of being seen as a fraud and fear of not being enough. Even when they called back a *second* time, I said "no." There was no way I could do it.

Twenty-two years later, I still present that seminar for the small community co-op's scholarship winners, but I will never forget the opportunity I passed up. And now that I speak regularly about various topics, it leaves me wondering what if I hadn't let my fear, shame, and lies get in my way.

Power Takeaways

I have found that the quickest way to gain confidence is to take action. Any step forward is a step toward success, and any step backward is still progress on what *not* to do next time.

- The lesson is to keep going, pushing yourself to do the work to gain that confidence, and creating goals along the way to help you improve your power of confidence.
- Realize that everyone, at some level, struggles with confidence—you are not alone.
- Identify the areas holding you back and align them with the WHY behind those areas.
- Get to the true root cause that is causing you to give way your confidence power, then identify whether it is out of fear, shame or just a lie you tell yourself. Doing so will give you direction to take action.

- Take action to then overcome those beliefs and establish a new frame of thinking to help you restore and build upon your power of confidence.

Power Thinking and Journaling

- What is holding back your confidence? Why are you not confident? Fear? Shame? Lies?
- What is your story, and how does it impact your actions?
- What action can you take today to help you own your power of confidence?

_____

_____

_____

_____

_____

_____

_____

_____

_____

_____

Books to Help You Own
Your Power of Confidence

Daring Greatly: How the Courage to Be Vulnerable Transforms the Way We Live, Love, Parent, and Lead by Brené Brown

Presence: Bringing Your Boldest Self to Your Biggest Challenges by Amy Cuddy

Feel the Fear … and Do It Anyway by Susan Jeffers

CHAPTER 3

The Power in Planning

"A goal without a plan is just a wish."

—Antoine de Saint-Exupéry, French writer, poet,
aristocrat, journalist, and pioneering aviator

Are You In The 3%?

When it comes to planning, it always seems you have two types
of people. The first type is the ultimate planner—everything is
planned out in life, organized in a tidy synchronized list with
little check boxes next to each item. The second type is the "let us
wing it and figure it out as we go" type. In reality, I think we all
are a little bit of each even if it is 95% one type and 5% the other;
we all have a little bit of both in us.

Failing to plan and have a direction for your life gives
away your power. Whether it is in your education, your career,
your community activities, or family obligations, having a plan
empowers you to achieve your goals.

However, motivational speaker and self-development author
Brian Tracy indicates less than 3% of us write down our goals.

Why is that?! When you consider psychologist, professor, and career coach Dr. Gail Matthews found that 61% of goals written down are achieved, the number of people who simply *write down their goals* should be much higher. "Begin with the end in mind," per Stephen Covey, educator, businessman, and world-renowned author of *The 7 Habits of Highly Effective People.* Therefore, take a few extra minutes a week or a month to focus on your endgame–your goals–and write them down; it can significantly impact your life.

Power Point

Take a few extra minutes a week or a month to focus on your endgame–your goals–and write them down; it can significantly impact your life.

"Impacting your life significantly"—now that is a bold statement. But, let us think about how your life would change if you put some structure around what you want to do in your life. It would be a roadmap to success—your personal road map.

Are You In Front of Your Goals?

If we needed to get to our favorite music artist's concert—a concert for which we paid quite a bit of money and that's taking place in a venue we've never visited before—do we just jump into the car, figure out the path on the way, hoping we get there in time? NO! We get directions and follow them, allotting time for the possibility of traffic and navigating the parking lot, and we know when the gates open to make sure we have plenty of time to find our seats, get drinks beforehand, and make sure we pick out memorabilia. Think about that.

We put more effort into getting to that concert than we do in directing our own lives.

Setting up goals and creating a path to achieve them will help you determine what decisions to make and what situations to avoid that can take you off-course. If it does not fit the plan, then you have a clear answer, and you gain traction in reaching your ultimate goal.

Having a plan of your goals in life is also a sure path to financial planning success as well. It may be tempting to start here first—to start with figuring out how to maximize your money situation and planning where every dollar should go because that's exciting and seems to have more appeal. But you must first start with planning for your life, then plan for your finances because, quite honestly, if you do not know where you want to lead your life, then how in the world can you determine your financial wellbeing? For those who have large sums of money or trust funds, this does not apply to you. But, for the rest of us, these are the facts—if you let your financial situation dictate your actions, then you will never get in front of your goals. You have to let your goals lead you, then focus on how you financially work to achieve your goals. It will help you determine where and how you spend your money and how you adjust your career path.

Power Point

If you let your financial situation dictate your actions, then you will never get in front of your goals.

Case in point: Throughout my life, I first created goals for my life then, to generate the finances that would position me to achieve those goals, I either changed jobs or I simultaneously worked two or three jobs. If I had not done this—plan for my life, then plan for my finances—then I would have repeated a cycle of stress and worry about money and financial issues that I witnessed growing up. And in hindsight, this course of action just made good sense given that, according to a 2017 *Business Wire* article, "83% of people that set financial goals feel better about their finances after just one year." When money is consistently listed as one of the highest factors that causes stress and that leads to future medical issues, it seems obvious to begin to release this worry by simply beginning to plan. So, if you take a few minutes of your life—get away from scrolling social media or binge watching your favorite show—and begin writing your goals, you will have a higher likelihood of achieving them and building a strong financial future.

Start to own your power by establishing goals in all areas of your life: personal, spiritual, academic, professional, familial, health, and financial. Ask yourself what is important to you and what you want to accomplish in each of those areas on a short-term, mid-term, and long-term basis. Short-term is within the next three months, mid-term is within the next year, and long-term is within the next five years. Use this chart to create your goals:

Goals	Social (family, friends, pets)	Spiritual (volunteering, community activities, self-care, ways you can give back)	Professional (work, school, networking)	Financial (budgeting, saving, investing)
Short-term				
Mid-term				
Long-term				

Next, evaluate your goals by asking yourself these questions:

- Are these goals really what I want to accomplish, or are they what a parent or a significant other thinks I should set and try to achieve?

  A goal must be something *you* desire to complete, and it is not designed or intended to please others. Your attitude and how you feel about accomplishing these goals are directly related to whether you achieve them or not, therefore, you must be personally invested in the goals, and they must be what *you* want to achieve, not what someone else has told you that you should do.
- Do I know the reason for each of the goals I created? Does each one truly make me happy? Does each goal help me reach a bigger piece of success and get me closer to achieving my life's purpose? (More on finding your purpose is covered in the next section of this chapter.)

  My dog, Boulder, a 130-pound Alaskan Malamute, has a very lofty goal. He wants to catch a car! How do

I know he has this goal? Because he almost rips my arm off, straining against his leash as I struggle to maintain a grip on it, as he tries to achieve this goal every day during his morning walk. However, the fact is if he were to ever catch the ever-elusive shiny object, truly, he would NOT be happy. He cannot chew the car, he can't eat it, and most likely, it might end his life.

Often, we are like Boulder, chasing shiny objects, thinking that is what we want, but what happens if we get it? Does it truly make us happy? Does this goal help us reach a bigger success that will lead to achieving our life's purpose?

Finding Your Purpose

Finding what you believe is your purpose is a personal journey. In my case it changed several times over the past forty years. And, just when I thought I was doing well and was achieving it, God laid on my heart to go in a different direction. Now, my purpose was mostly outside of my career. It helped what I did during the business day but was never directly related to my job. So do not think your purpose is always directly aligned with your 9-to-5 job. It could be outside of that, in conjunction with, or directly aligned. We will cover about the power of faith in the next chapter, which is what I used to discern my purpose, but I have used various other techniques over the years to try to navigate this daunting task.

- **Where do you find your energy and motivation?**
  I noticed that some days at work were better than others, and it related to where I focused my energy. If I was able to solve a problem or help someone, it was a good

day for me even if it didn't have tangible results that one could immediately see. My husband, however, is the total opposite, he gets his joy from task completion. If he can get projects completed or tasks done, he is energized. Finding where you derive your energy, motivation, and happiness helps direct you toward this path of purpose.

- **What are your interests, skills, or talents?**
Are these just things you are good at, or are they what you feel makes you complete or at your calmest? Could you use those to fulfill a purpose that invigorates you?

- **Where do you find your calm?**
Go to this place, or do this activity, and focus on some self-reflection of what your purpose could be whether it is for where you are at in this current stage of your life or if there is a greater purpose you are looking for overall.

- **Do you notice patterns or things that keep reoccurring that are lending you towards a direction?**
Here is an example: I was contemplating if I should write this book. I felt for three years everything had been leading up to me writing it when the opportunity came out of the blue. But, was I understanding this correctly? Debating doing this, I was, once again, sitting at a coffee shop patio when a colleague called me. It was a large patio with only one other person, and she was working; so I felt I could take the call. When I got off the call, once again, the young lady who was on the patio approached me and stated "I didn't mean to eavesdrop on your conversation, but you sound like you give really good advice; and I need help with a work conflict I am having. Can I ask your advice?" For the next hour, we sat there, and I used techniques that I have included in this book to help her. That was my final sign—this pattern of total strangers seeking out my advice—and I said "yes" to the book.

- **Where are you the happiest? Who are you with, and what are you doing?**

  Are you engaging in activities that make you happy? And are you with people who make you the better version of you? Do they elevate you to reach your goals, or are they holding you back? Do you find joy in ways that could fulfill your purpose?

Reflecting on your purpose and making sure you are aligning with your goals accordingly will help you in ultimately owning your power.

- **Why am I setting this goal? Does my goal help me achieve the reason for setting that goal?**

  To understand this set of questions, let's examine a hypothetical. A young lady sets a goal of getting married by the age of twenty-eight. Is this woman directly in charge of her goal? Does her goal achieve what she truly wants to accomplish if she does in fact accomplish the goal? And aside from matrimony, is she clear on what it is she truly wants? Maybe, but maybe not. As she quickly approaches this random age she selected, she makes sacrifices in her quest to pick her significant other and ends up settling to reach a goal when in actuality, her true purpose is to have established herself as an independent and strong woman by the age of twenty-eight. Therefore, what she really wants is to be financially fit before getting married and to make sure she is emotionally ready for a commitment to last a lifetime.

  Therefore, instead of setting a goal of getting married by the age of twenty-eight, a goal that reaches her true purpose would be one that has taking actions that position her to earn the money she needs to reach a state of financial fitness or one that has her seeking out counsel, direction, and advice that prepare her for married life. Therefore, instead of putting a number or a date on a goal that she only half controls and that calls for her to make questionable sacrifices, she can put a date on a goal she fully owns and that reaches her true purpose.

- **Is my goal specific enough to precisely measure it?**
I am the SPIN MASTER!! I can spin anything in my head to say I achieved it. I often laugh at myself, especially with my health goals, when I try to convince myself that I achieved the goals I set. I fall into the trap of not being specific enough or not being able to measure it. For example, "I will begin to eat healthy" is a short-term goal I set with no specifics around it. So, after thirty days, when I step back to assess how I did, that means I drank one less soda that month. Woohoo! There's a checkmark on my goal to begin to eat healthy! But, in actuality, that does NOTHING for me. *So what* if I accomplished that lazy goal! Does it truly get me closer to reaching my end desire? The answer is clear—NO. Not at all! I know soda makes me feel run down and does nothing to help my focus and attention, so reducing my consumption of it was a plus.

  However, I need to write down that goal in a way that makes it specific enough to measure so I can better position myself to reach my ultimate goal of eating healthier. With that in mind, my updated short-term goal is "I will eliminate soda from my diet for the next thirty days." That's precise and measurable. And little by little, each month, it worked! Now, I'm to the point where I might have a total of one soda once a year.

- **Did I share my goals with anyone?**
I am not one to often share as it has not always ended up as pleasant, but there is power in sharing goals.

Science Daily published a research article from Ohio State University indicating that when you share your goals with others, you become more likely to achieve them. It drives accountability for yourself, and often those you share it with hold you accountable as well. This is how it works: You run into a person at the store—a person you hold in high regard—and they ask you "How is your training for the 5K going?" You then remember you shared your goal with them, and now you are further driven to achieve the goal of training for the 5K.

It is important the type of person with whom you share certain goals. Sharing a goal with someone you look up to helps you keep the goal because, internally, you do not want to let them down. Having the extra accountability to complete your goals is the emphasis behind this idea. At the same time, you may share other goals with someone who is supportive and caring enough to want you to succeed and who will help drive accountability.

Sometimes it is helpful to share a goal with someone who is critical or who might be very different from yourself. If you are confident in your goal and committed and you really want someone to be that nay-sayer to ensure you have thought through every issue that could arise, then you want to share with that critical person. But, recall chapter 1, and go into the conversation of sharing your goal with the power of understanding; doing so will only make you plan to achieve your goal that much stronger.

- **Am I actively reviewing and assessing my goals?**
When you regularly track your progress, it keeps your goals front of mind. Yes, life gets busy, and everyday commitments to your job or school, family, and friends

get overwhelming; but dedicating just a few minutes a week to review and assess your goals is an important part in achieving them. And DO NOT STOP THERE! Always have your sights set on what's next. Take it from the late author, salesman, and motivational speaker Zig Ziegler: "What you get by achieving your goals is not as important as what you BECOME by achieving your goals." You accomplished a goal—GREAT! Now, what's the next one? How are you evolving as a person? What will you do next to be even better?

- **Are my goals still relevant?**
  Your goals are not the Ten Commandments. They are NOT set in stone. Your goals adapt with you as you change and evolve. Goals you set that seem relevant today can change in a year because life throws you curve balls. New opportunities present themselves, and we decide to take different paths. And that is okay. In fact, that is better than okay—that is AWESOME because it means you are owning your power. You are making decisions, making plans, and taking control of your next steps.

Are You In the Driver's Seat?

Once you own your power through planning, setting goals, and finding a path to achieve those goals, make sure you incorporate planning in *all* areas of your life. Too often, we venture into new situations without conducting the proper research and planning to be successful, and in that lack of planning, we give away our power. For the sake of illustration, we will examine a common situation that *should* involve planning but ... well ... it doesn't always happen.

Making a large purchase such as buying a new car is stressful. In fact, in research conducted with 1,000 Americans, most said buying a car was more stressful than getting married or going on a first date! With this situation being so stressful, why do people not fully research or plan their own expectations before stepping foot in a dealership or going online to buy a car? By avoiding this step, the car buyer immediately gives away their power to the dealership or to the car seller because now they are in a situation where the seller can greatly influence their buying power. Going in with little to no knowledge about automobiles, financing, what to expect, or the process can lead to the buyer being easily persuaded and possibly duped into making a bad purchase.

Here is just a sampling of questions to consider and answer before engaging with a vehicle seller so you can truly own your power as you walk into this stressful situation:

- Why do I need a car? What will I use it for?
- How much can I afford to pay (lump sum or monthly payments)?
- How much can I afford on gas each week? How much do I drive, therefore, what kind of gas mileage do I need in a car?
- Do I have any concerns about where my money is spent or concern about the environment? Do I care about domestic or foreign brands? Will I consider an electric or a hybrid vehicle?
- How much can I afford for insurance?
- What maintenance costs can I afford on a monthly or annual basis?

Once you ask these questions and answer them honestly, these answers should help you focus your search. And once you find a car, you have to research by answering additional questions to make sure it fits to your answers above!

- What year is the car? Based on its age, are there any repairs needed now or in the next year that I must financially plan for? And if so, what are those costs? (i.e., tires, brakes, etcetera.)
- What type of gas does it take? (i.e., Certain makes and models require premium. Premium costs more and might not fit with your budget.)
- What is the gas mileage?
- What does general maintenance cost? (oil change, tire rotation, etcetera).
- Are there any known recalls or associated issues that I might need to account for financially?
- What is the cost/monthly payment? And if not paying for the car in full, for how long will I have to make payments before the car is paid off? Do I even plan to pay it off? And in either instance, what is the next plan?
- How much is the insurance each month for this car on a monthly, bi-annual, or annual basis (while keeping in mind the shorter the term, the higher the premium)?
- How much will my sales tax be for this car, and when will I need to pay it?
- How much is registration? Will I roll it into the total financed amount of the car or pay it upfront?

Now, there are many more questions you could ask and answer, but these basics will position you to own your power when going into the highly stressful situation of buying a car. I know some amazing car salespeople and trust them completely, and you may feel the same. However, at the end of the day, it is NOT their responsibility to make sure this is the best car or best value for you—it is yours. Their job is to sell you a car. Period. Owning your power through this process puts you in the driver's seat—no pun intended!

Now that you got into the specifics on this one example of buying a car, how can you make a modified list for other big decisions like changing jobs, moving across the country or even where to go on vacation? Each list will be different, but in broad strokes, you are dealing with the same method of planning before you act. This doesn't have to be a long, drawn-out process. Sometimes it is just weighing pros and cons with a mental checklist.

- Why am I making this decision?
- Does it align with my goals and what goal is this helping me fulfill?
- Does this align with my values and my brand?
- Are there others to consider in my decision? How are they impacted? Does it matter?
- What is my financial responsibility for this decision?
- What risks do I face when making this decision?
- How does this decision impact my future goals?
- What specifics do I need to research before I can make this decision?
- If I don't make this decision, how am I impacted?

Research and take this approach for all major decisions in your life whether it is buying a house, deciding what college to attend, changing careers, or even deciding what pet you should own. You might laugh at the last one, but according to a 2020 article released by the National Center of Biotechnology, a division of the National Institutes of Health's National Library of Medicine, returns of animals post-adoption or post-purchase are estimated to be as high as 20% with some of the reasons for returns being associated with owners not fully understanding the needs—whether financial or physical—of the breed or the type of pet purchased. The point? Leave no stone unturned when it comes to planning.

You Do Not Have to Be 100% Qualified for the Job

After all this hype around planning, this may come as a surprise, but you do not have to be 100% qualified before you apply for a position! Yes, your skills need to match the position requirements on some levels; for instance, you cannot have a background of working in airport security, see a position for a university athletic director, and while you are able to check none of the skill boxes, you decide to apply, nonetheless. Yes, some skills may be transferable, and yes, you *can* apply, however, the likelihood you'll get a call back is next to nil.

The point is you should look at the qualifications and quickly know you have the ability to do the work even if you may have to do some learning along the way, and be able to articulate in the interview process why you are qualified for the position. Place more emphasis on your strengths than on your shortcomings. As a matter of fact, do not mention a gap in your skills unless it comes up, and even then, assess whether it is indeed a gap, then if it is, address it by providing your plan for closing the gap. In doing so, you secure and own your power.

Before going into the interview, though, and after identifying the position that sounds like the perfect fit, even go so far as to evaluate whether the company you selected to work for would be a good fit as well. Examine its mission, vision, and core values and how well they match yours, learn about the culture and how well the company respects work-life balance, or find out what kind of commitment the company has to the growth and professional development of its employees. Do your research.

I recently mentored a secondary educator who was moving from being a teacher to becoming a tech sales professional. When we first met, she did not realize all her skillsets that she could transfer from the classroom to become a successful woman in tech sales. First, we outlined her most important skillsets she used every day in teaching secondary students. Next, we applied them to the business world, then specifically to a role in sales. After that, we talked about what type of companies she wanted to work for. How would the company, its corporate culture, and their products align to her goals, her beliefs, her interests, and most importantly, how does the company's values align to her personal values? Next, she took the initiative to complete special trainings, listen to podcasts, and read articles focused on the sales position and the companies she was interested in. All this planning took a few months, but from her last day of teaching until the day she received her first job offer that fit her criteria, less than a month had passed! She owned her power of planning and turned it into reaching her goals.

Then there was the instance of an entrepreneur who engaged with several venture capital (VC) companies to secure start-up money. His idea was really solid—it helped his local community's economy, it brought in new jobs, it helped with a product shortage, and he was excited to get started. One investor he talked to was pretty arrogant and called him out on the value and mission of his company, pointing out that the entrepreneur's focus was to make an impact and that to help the local economy and increase jobs was noble, but at the end of the day, he also stood to also make a great deal of income—so, long story short, is he really just doing it for the money? Well, this entrepreneur knew the power of planning. He had thoroughly researched every VC company he was talking to, prepping before each meeting so he would be ready for anything. As such, he quickly came back with the best answer ever. He pointed out that that may very well be the case, that he could stand to make a handsome profit, and hopefully both happens, that he helps the community while simultaneously earning a bit of cash; but in the end, it is not any different than how a VC invests its money compared to its mission and values. And to support this point, he went on to specifically point out several investments that aligned to that fact. The investor couldn't deny how great of an answer that was, and the meeting proceeded favorably. The entrepreneur owned his power that day—by leveraging the power of planning.

Power Point

Be ready for anything.

Power Takeaways

Now I know the excuses—who has time to do all this planning? The actual truth is you do! The hours you waste on your pursuits, spinning wheels without planning will far outnumber the hours of success and forward movement on your goals that come from you engaging in adequate planning. And to be honest, I must have these same real conversations with myself often. Scroll ten minutes less on social media ... watch one less Netflix show ... be more productive during downtime or while commuting. (Some of my best time to plan is while I am driving. No, I am not writing, but I turn on my voice recorder and engage the voice-to-text functionality on my phone to track my ideas or thoughts.) It does not take long to invest into yourself, just a few minutes a day.

Plan your goals, plan your purchases, plan your career, plan as best as you can for the outcomes you want in the end. It does not mean that it will all work out perfectly; there are no guarantees. But it does mean that you owned your power, did not leave everything to chance, and that you did everything you can to help get the results you envisioned.

The power of planning simply takes some of your time and follows the steps as outlined in this chapter.

- Establish your goals for all aspects of your life: social, professional, spiritual, and financial.
- In establishing your goals make certain they align with your personal brand and/or your greater purpose.
- Next, create a plan to achieve those goals with specific actions.
- Finally, make sure when you make decisions to own your power of planning that you don't get off-course with your goals. By failing to plan, you give your power away.

Power Thinking and Journaling

- Have you owned your power through planning?
- Do you have your goals established for all areas of your life?
- In what ways can you improve your power of planning?
- How can you take immediate action today to own your power of planning?

_____

_____

_____

_____

_____

_____

_____

_____

_____

Books to Help You Own
Your Power in Planning

The Richest Man in Babylon George Samuel Clason

The 7 Habits of Highly Effective People by Stephen Covey

The Power of Owning Your Career by Simone E. Morris

CHAPTER 4

The Power in Faith

*"Faith is taking the first step even when you don't
see the whole staircase."*

—Rev. Dr. Martin Luther King, Jr.,
American Baptist minister, activist, and civil rights leader

What Works for You May
Not Work for Them

Having faith in yourself is one of the hardest obstacles to face. It's having intuition or a gut reaction—you know that feeling you get deep inside that gives you direction. I have always felt that when my gut is telling me something good or bad, it's a sign from God. I have faith not only in Him but also in myself to have discernment—whether it is a big move like changing jobs or a small one like which route to take on the way home. When I have failed to trust my gut, I failed! It has always come to haunt me, and it's haunted me repeatedly. As such, I know to always trust my gut and have faith.

In 2012 or so, I was sharing aspirational goals with a person I trusted and in what I felt was a safe space to share. I am not going to lie—they were some lofty goals—but it was something I had prayed on and that I felt compelled to put forth an action plan to set them into motion. After I excitedly shared the full scope of how I set the goals to how I created the plan of action, the person replied with "If you think that is going to happen, you are as dumb as a box of rocks."

Now, that comment hit like a punch to the stomach. It literally took the breath right out of me, and I silently teared up. I quickly left the room to calm down. In my mind, I took a step back to first view the conversation from their perspective. My assessment revealed that this is not someone who really goes after large goals; this is someone who plays it safe. That works well for them, and in their mind, they felt as if they were trying to be rational because in their current state of life, from their vantage point, the goals I had set forth were completely unimaginable and totally out of reach … for them. The difference between the two of us was not only did I have goals, but I had faith, I had a plan, and I was willing to put in the work.

Taking deep, heavy breaths to calm myself, I gathered my thoughts and proceeded with my day. However, I did not let their opinion deter me, and to be honest, I didn't let it impact my relationship with them either. I accepted them for who they were and knew they meant well with their words. I moved forward; however, I learned the cautionary tale of not sharing any future goals with that person.

I felt confident in the goals and the action plan to reach the goals, but most importantly, I had faith. Faith it until you make it. I truly felt God called me in the direction He was taking me with my career, and I had faith in myself to achieve or adjust accordingly. I am happy to report that those goals were achieved and have continued to grow and compound into new goals and additional opportunities.

Power Point

Faith it until you make it.

Trust Your Gut

Multiple opportunities will come your way, and my advice is to always JUMP! It could be the decision to jump head-on and face your fears; trust your gut and take that leap. If it is truly where you think you should be and what you should do, it will work out one way or another. Or your gut might be telling you to jump back—avoid the freight train coming down those tracks and choose not to go forward. Either way, it is FANTASTIC because it was *your* choice. Know that whatever path you take, it is right, and you will figure out how to navigate it.

Power Point

Whatever path you take, it is right, and you will figure out how to navigate it.

Navigating how to trust my gut isn't always easy. What if you think it is your gut or it is fear or self-doubt creeping in? Or, what if it is something distracting and bad for you, but you think it is your gut. For me, I feel my gut is my conscience and my guiding principle is my faith in God. As I have shared before, my Christian beliefs are a guiding principle for me. The first four books of the Bible's New Testament are historical accounts of the life of Jesus. (Quick background: Christians believe that Jesus is the Son of God, as prophesied in the Old Testament, who was sent as the perfect sacrifice [John 3:16].) What I find so intriguing in these historical accounts of Jesus is that each time Jesus performs a miracle, the Bible does not include statements from Jesus such as, "I have healed you" or "My Father has healed you." Instead, there is a focus on the person's faith or the belief of what healed them. (This is beautifully illustrated in Matthew 9:27-31; Mark 5:34; and Luke 18:42.) It's one's faith from within that is given the credit.

I had an opportunity to make a career change, and recognizing the power in faith would play a significant role. It was a position with duties I unequivocally knew I could execute well, but I questioned the company culture. Even before the first interview, I knew it would not be a good fit, however, my thought process was if I was allowed to apply my personal leadership style and vision, then it would be an experience I could really enjoy. Even in my final contract negotiations, my gut and my faith told me to take the position when all common sense told me to run. I remember thinking to myself "God, this is going to be a learning moment, isn't it?"

And it was.

I learned that my personal brand and value outweigh any leadership title or position, that the value I bring to the table is not always recognized, but that doesn't mean it is not of value; and those who do not see it are not people I care to impress, especially when we are not ethically aligned. And finally—I realized this just when I needed it—I had an amazing network of colleagues and friends willing to support me as I navigated this.

A lesson I learned is you never know who is watching you, the moves you make and the decisions you choose. People called me out of nowhere when things were taking a turn for me in that position—people ranging from past leaders that once mentored me to new individuals that I had recently met. They all reached out to tell me that that role might have sounded impressive, but it truly would never value my skill set and that I had so much to offer.

Power Point

The value you bring to the table may not always be recognized, but that does not mean it is not of value.

I realized, my brand and the path I established along the way supported me when I needed it the most because I made an impact on individuals. So even though it would have been easier to pass on that job, I trusted my gut and had faith. Even though it was painful, it was also a rewarding experience that helped me jump into a greater calling, which I would have never known without this slight career detour. I would have never had the guts to even write this book. Wouldn't it be so much easier in life if God just sent you a text message that read "Sit tight. I have a plan"? Well, the power of faith is knowing He doesn't need to send that because it is always true. Now as I reflect, I see the beautiful masterpiece God continues to create in my life as I continue to work on my power of faith.

Know When to Let Go

To utilize your power of faith means you also know when to let an opportunity or a situation go, especially when you cannot control it. When you carry a worry and a burden that causes stress, it steals away your power. If you know the cause of a pain, it seems the smart thing to do is to get rid of the source of the discomfort. When what to do to improve your circumstance is right in front of your face, it only makes sense that you help yourself. God helps those who help themselves, right? This is great advice to follow, and I believe there is truth in the saying, but here is the real truth: That quote appears nowhere in the Bible nor is any variation of it mentioned anywhere in the Good Book, thus God did not say that. Benjamin Franklin did in 1757, the English political theorist Algernon Sidney said it in the early 1600s, and it is illustrated in two Aesop's Fables. Nonetheless, regardless of its origin, it's still good advice if followed correctly when faced with worries: help yourself by letting go of the stressor.

Letting go of that stressor is often easier if we are the cause of the stress or if it is just a small inconvenience. For those who have endured great hardships or who have been victims of injustice in this world, it can be difficult to own your power of faith if you are truly powerless. This brings to mind the story of Joseph in the Old Testament, which some may know from the Broadway production *Joseph and the Amazing Technicolor Dreamcoat*. (Please note the two stories are not one in the same.)

Joseph's brothers, consumed by jealousy, beat him and threw him into a pit. They then sold him into slavery, and he eventually found himself imprisoned after being falsely accused of a crime. How does one find strength in the face of such constant adversity and abuse? Joseph's unwavering faith and trust in God's plan for his life helped him endure. Despite his circumstances, he never lost sight of his values or his beliefs. Eventually, Joseph earned favor with the Pharaoh and became his trusted advisor, which ultimately led to him saving his family from famine—the very same family that had sold him into slavery.

Joseph's story is a powerful reminder that even in the face of immense hardship one can still find strength in their faith and the belief that a higher power has a plan for them. Through determination and resilience, one can persevere and overcome even the most daunting challenges. Joseph's faith never wavered in his troubles—he was never the hero; he always just trusted God to be the hero of his story. In comparison to Joseph, I have only had minor worries in my life. But to me, they were still too big for me to "help myself" to truly fix them; I needed faith to help me get through it.

Being a Christian, I was told to leave your worries at the foot of the cross for it is written in Isaiah 25:4 that God is a place a refuge: "For you have been a stronghold to the poor, a stronghold to the needy in his distress, a shelter from the storm and a shade from the heat; for the breath of the ruthless is like a storm against a wall." And Psalm 55:22 asserts we are to "Cast your burden on the Lord ..." But this left me wondering. What does that mean to leave your worries at the cross? How does one do that? And can I not pick them back up?

Leaving a worry at the foot of cross is simply releasing it, saying "This is no longer my worry. This is yours, God" and having faith to not go back and try to pick it up, truly letting go and placing your faith in a force or an authority that is stronger than your ability to control a situation.

Matthew 11: 28-30 states this clearly: [28]Come to me, all you who labor and are heavy laden, and I will give you rest. [29]Take my yoke upon you and learn from me, for I am gentle and lowly in heart, and you will find rest for your souls. [30]For my yoke is easy and my burden is light.

And every time I do this, I feel a lightness from my heart. It is still a struggle for me, especially when things are going well. I know that sounds crazy! But, when I am at a low point, I have nowhere to go but to God and to trust in Him, and God is always faithful in His promise to provide. But, when I am doing well and I hit a slight snag, that is when it is the hardest for me to have faith. And I have come to find out that is completely natural to try to control an outcome and not be too hard on myself. But at the same time, it does not qualify as an excuse for me to not own my power of faith.

Forgiveness is for You, Not the Person You're Forgiving

When you hold on to anger and resentment toward others, you do not own your faith. Period. This is another area where you own your power of faith—through forgiveness, forgiving yourself as well as forgiving others. But we mistakenly feel that by holding on to anger and resentment, we protect ourselves from getting hurt again. Or maybe we don't think the other person deserves forgiveness, but forgiving them is not really for them. It is for you and for your faith in yourself to move forward. Forgiveness is not about freeing the other person from owning any part of the transgression; it's about freeing yourself from holding onto and possibly being paralyzed by the transgression or being paralyzed by your feelings surrounding it and/or the transgressor. It's about freeing you, not the other person.

Power Point

Forgiveness is not about freeing the other person from owning any part of the transgression; it's about freeing yourself.

I was raised by strong women, and I am very fortunate in many ways; however, forgiving my father for being absent was one of the longest processes I have undergone. My parents divorced when I was just two years old, and I rarely saw him. I buried the feelings, ignored the pain that I felt, and never dealt with either one. As a child, I saw him periodically, and as I grew older, I did my best to travel and take my kids to see him, never mentioning anything of substance regarding my feelings. Over the years, I realized I had forgiven him in my heart and that I had the faith to forgive him without him ever owning up to the part he played in the creation of my pain.

In 2010, he underwent a medical procedure that did not go as planned and resulted in his heart stopping for more than thirty minutes. During that week while he was on life support, family members took turns sitting with and talking to him. When it was my turn to sit with him, I decided to have that conversation. Even though I had forgiven him, I needed him to know. I shared with him stories of my childhood, how it felt with him not being there, and what it was like seeing him be a father to my step- and half siblings but never to me. Nonetheless, in the end, I told him that I had forgiven him long ago. I told him I had no regrets because I have been blessed with an amazing life, and I was just happy he was a great granddad to my children. As I finished talking and holding his hand, a tear fell from his left eye and ran down his cheek. It made me smile, and I truly felt a release from my chest as I felt a lightness surround me. I let the nurse know in case it meant his brain activity had changed; but she simply stated it was a normal body reaction for the eyes water, and it wasn't anything of significance. But this was the very first and only time that week that that happened, so for me, I took it as something—I took it as a sign of closure. Two days later and three minutes after being taken off life support, he passed away.

Shortly after his passing, while having dinner with his sister, I told her about the moment in the hospital. And she said, "You know, he once told me something in confidence that I feel I can now share with you. Your Dad stated that his greatest accomplishment was staying out of your life because of how amazing you turned out. He saw something different in you and did not want to mess it up."

Wow!

I was taken aback.

If only I had been strong enough to have the faith to engage in conversations with him earlier, then I could have gained that understanding and even possibly helped him not feel that way.

Power Takeaways

Faith to have that hard conversations, to be vulnerable if needed, is scary. Not knowing how things will turn out, being guarded, and playing it safe have rarely ended in greatness. And why be mediocre when we can be a better version of ourselves?

- Let go of your worries and doubts.
- Place a belief in the plans you have created, trust in your decisions, and learn when to let go. This is how you own your power of faith.

Power Thinking and Journaling

- Do you have gut instincts? If yes, do you listen to them or ignore them?
- Do you have faith or an optimistic mindset?
- What areas can you explore to own your power of faith?

_____

_____

_____

_____

_____

_____

_____

_____

_____

_____

Books to Help You Own
Your Power of Faith

The Reason for God: Belief in an Age of Skepticism by Timothy Keller

It's Not Supposed to Be This Way: Finding Unexpected Strength When Disappointments Leave You Shattered by Lysa TerKeurst

The Purpose Driven Life: What on Earth Am I Here For? By Rick Warren

CHAPTER 5

The Power in Adaptability

"We cannot direct the wind, but we can adjust the sails."

—Dolly Parton, American singer-songwriter, actress, philanthropist, and businesswoman

It's Up to You How You Handle Feedback

When I was in my mid-twenties, I was so excited to get promoted to a project manager role. I was organized, was not afraid to ask questions, thought quickly on my feet, and did not shy away from holding cross-functional teams or individuals accountable for deliverables.

Approximately one year into the role, it was time to receive my annual performance review. The company, at that time, brought together the groups' directors, and the directors reviewed and evaluated each employee's performance based on a scale, then provided feedback to help the employee with growth and development. When I met with my director, I was excited with my review, then she proceeded to share something that another director had mentioned. She was reluctant at first, and I could tell in her hesitation she was concerned with how to approach the topic. She finally shared that that director felt that I came across as very intimidating in meetings and presentations. She told me that I *did* ask hard questions, and I drove accountability in the projects that I led; so I could take the feedback how I would like, but it was ultimately up to me how I handled the feedback.

To say the least, I was flabbergasted!

To me, I felt like I was this little girl, and who in the world could ever be intimidated by me?! I was one of the youngest by far in the position, had not finished my college education yet, and was literally at a loss as to why someone in his position would feel that way about me. So, as I did quite often, I went home and discussed with my husband how to take this feedback.

My husband shocked me.

He stated, "You are not intimidating. He is intimidated by you. There is no need to change. Hold your ground and continue your approach." It's likely the director's thinking was "How dare someone so young have the audacity to be so confident?!" And his way of articulating it in the form of performance review nomenclature was to say I was intimidating. I felt validated at first, but ultimately, I did NOT take my husband's advice even though I know it came from a place of love and support.

Adapt to feedback and make yourself stronger mentally; in the end, that is how you own your power. So, I owned the fact that I was intimidating to some, and I started to research the best way to approach this feedback so I could achieve more in each project I implemented without losing my passion and diluting my inquisitive mindset. My intent was positive, but somewhere along the way, because of my approach, this was getting lost.

Power Point

Adapt to feedback and make yourself
stronger mentally; in the end, that is how
you own your power.

Before I tell you how I found my way, here is one clear conclusion and viewpoint on what it means to have a successful life: A direct correlation exists between how you achieve success and the way you change and adapt as a person. For this discussion on adaptability, defining the term "success" is quite important because it can be interpreted differently, and depending on this interpretation, the ability to truly feel fulfilled with a successful life can be impacted.

Power Point

A direct correlation exists between how
you achieve success and the way you change
and adapt as a person.

Oftentimes, people see success as acquiring a large sum of money, achieving a level of fame, amassing all kinds of possessions, or gaining a certain number of social media followers.

But that is insufficient for defining "success" or achieving a successful life. That does not mean those are not commendable; it's that none of them adequately and ultimately defines "success."

Success is the ability to execute what you were put on this earth to achieve, to truly be fulfilled, and serving the purpose you were meant to fulfil. Success is being able to answer the ultimate question "What is my purpose?" as well as being able to say "I am waking up every day and working towards that purpose." For me, that means following what God has called me to do—that is living a successful life. And guess what—that calling or purpose continues to grow and evolve, and if we do not continue to grow and evolve as well, we might never reach our full potential.

Power Point

Success is the ability to execute what you were put on this earth to achieve, to truly be fulfilled, and serving the purpose you were meant to fulfil.

When you grow and evolve, it does not mean you change your core beliefs or your preferred activities, but growth and evolution help you better understand why others think and act the way they do. Being able to adapt makes you more well-rounded; it gets you out of your comfort zone and opens your eyes to acknowledge and respect other points of view. It does not mean you agree with those who disagree with you or who offer unpopular or questionable opinions; it simply means you are able to more easily adjust and stretch your outlook, and eventually, this reduces stress and anxiety when life throws you a curveball.

So, as I worked to leverage the "intimidating" feedback, I dove into conducting research, and I found out that most often this type of disconnect happens as a result of a difference in communication styles. How someone is perceived can be based on how they communicate, and if it is a style that differs from that of the recipient of the information, it can come across in an unintended way, thus, impeding the main message and its true intent from reaching the listener. The conclusion I drew was my communication style caused that director to view me as intimidating.

So, next, I started to investigate these different communication styles. There are a ton of books and assessments on this topic, but ultimately, there are about four distinctive communication styles; and while a person can be a combination of styles, each person typically leans towards one particular style. One of the styles I researched was the DiSC assessment. You can learn more by visiting discprofile.com. DiSC is an acronym for the four main personality profiles described in the DiSC model: (D)ominance, (i)nfluence, (S)teadiness, and (C)onscientiousness. According to the DiSC website …

People with D personalities tend to be confident and place an emphasis on accomplishing bottom-line results.

People with i personalities tend to be more open and place an emphasis on relationships and influencing or persuading others.

People with S personalities tend to be dependable and place an emphasis on cooperation and sincerity.

People with C personalities tend to place an emphasis on quality, accuracy, expertise, and competency.

Assess your style or combination of styles to identify how you give and receive information. Once you effectively analyze another person's communication style, quickly adapt your style in an effort to match theirs. The point is the better you can adapt your communication, the greater the likelihood you will be able to better get along. For instance, if you have a C personality, when met with someone who has a D personality, place less emphasis on your expertise and more emphasis on the bottom line.

I quickly began to adapt my communication style based on what I learned, and ultimately, it was noticed and received very well by not only the one director who gave the "intimidating" feedback, but I noticed positive shifts in my career and how I was able to more effectively accomplish team tasks. As I look back, if I had never accepted this little bit of feedback and owned my power to learn and adapt, if I had chosen to ignore it or worse yet, if I had chosen to be upset and let my anger get in the way of me learning from it, I am positive my career would not have had the same positive trajectory.

Years later, I took the DiSC assessment again and assumed the results would be quite different given I had evolved so much as a human. But nope—the results were the same. The fact is you are who you are; that never changes. It's what you do with the information you learn about yourself that results in you making changes and growing as a person.

Power Point

You are who you are; that never changes. It's what you do with the information you learn about yourself that results in you making changes and growing as a person.

My passion for exploring how communication styles differ took me down a path of leadership development, leading through change, and ultimately discovering how diverse teams create more lucrative results. Diversity is more than surface deep like race or gender—although they are significantly important. Diversity includes age, seniority, socio-economic background, geography, work history, education level, and many more differences. Creating a diverse team leads to diversity of thought, but a challenge is that oftentimes, it is harder to relate to someone who is different and who may communicate differently than you. I quickly learned how important it is to understand your own motivations as well as the motivations of others while also paying attention to how each person communicates.

Think of someone you do not get along with or who seems drastically different than you. What motivates them? How can you adapt to reach common ground? Let's get those answers.

Can We Talk About This Drink?!

While I was facilitating a college course, we dug into this topic of communication styles, and I loved bringing real world examples into the class. This particular class was a master's level business communications course, and one student, Thomas, was a manager for an insurance company. As we talked about how to work as a team, and he brought up a team member with whom he worked and whom he believed was his workplace arch nemesis. He could not stand to work with this woman and felt she was an obstacle in getting anything done. He was adamant that she needed to voluntarily leave the company or be fired. As a class, we analyzed Thomas's communication style, and based on Thomas's descriptions, we also analyzed his co-worker's communication style.

We quickly assessed that they had completely opposite communication styles. (Shocker!!) As a class and with my direction, we put forth actions for Thomas to take over the next few weeks in to adapt to his arch nemesis' communication style. The goal was to see if it would change the team environment.

Two weeks later, Thomas marched into class and enthusiastically slammed an energy drink down on my desk. With a smirk on his face, he said, "Can we talk about this drink before our lesson this week?" Intrigued by his enthusiasm, I was excited to hear his story. You see, Thomas shared that his favorite beverage was this particular energy drink and that this very can had been given to him that very day by none other than … his arch nemesis!

Thomas took his class assignment seriously and implemented the adapted communication style. He felt it was working and was quickly able to adjust to not only the woman he detested but to others on the team as well. And this change did not go unnoticed! His arch nemesis told him she did not know what had changed but that she had begun to enjoy working with him and really appreciated how much he was trying to be different. She noticed he enjoyed a certain energy drink, so she wanted to buy him one to simply say "Thank you!" Thomas was beaming! He was happier at work as well. He stated it was not that hard to adapt, that it felt good to get the team projects done without a fuss, and he even implemented the adaptations at home with friends and family.

Remember the student from chapter 1, Dante? He had a similar ending to his story. He applied our lessons on being open to fully listening to others and embracing compromises. He looked beyond himself for meaning in what others said and embraced compromises by eliminating a focus on being the one who was right and instead used communication where both sides make concessions to reach a mutually agreeable solution. Later that year, after he completed my class, he reached out via LinkedIn, sharing that by applying these practices, it landed him a promotion with a relocation to another city, a new adventure about which he was excited.

What do these stories have in common? These two gentlemen, both from very different backgrounds working in different industries at different stages of their lives, put their egos aside and made changes as needed. They adapted and owned their power to push their careers forward. Ultimately, the truth is they were coachable! They were open to learning, growing, and evolving.

There is no faster way to give away your power than to not be coachable. Not being coachable hinders you from being able to adapt. When you are open to coaching, you are open to taking accountability for your actions, even if there is nothing wrong with your intent but that you need to better understand the perspectives of others.

Power Point

There is no faster way to give away your power than to not be coachable.

She Expected a Fight

Not long after getting the "intimidating" feedback, I continued to apply new techniques to my communication style to more effectively look for the intent and motivations of others, and these techniques were soon put to the test.

I was on a business trip with my boss when she received a call and abruptly left to handle it while I was on the operations floor, reviewing some project details. She came back to the floor and asked me to join her in an available office. The call she had just received was from the project systems manager about the project I was running, and that manager felt I had erroneously pointed blame at her team. I quickly listened to the feedback, and I realized the issue. Often while traveling, I try to get emails done quickly in the airport or while temporarily connected to Wi-Fi, and the email message in question was a message composed and sent under such circumstances. It was in that instance that I could see how her point of view; I could see how it was possible for her to read blame in the message that I'd composed a little too quickly although to assign blame was not my intent. And in that moment, I took ownership and asked if we could call the project systems manager. Together we called, I took ownership of the issue, and indicated I would send a follow-up clarification email if needed.

Now, technically, there was nothing wrong with the initial email I sent; however, I saw the project systems manager's point of view, and I saw how my email message was open to multiple interpretations. I did not apologize, but I did take ownership that the message could have been worded better or more clearly. I left the office for the remainder of the conversation and returned to the operations floor.

Approximately ten minutes later, my boss came out with a smile. She proclaimed, "You just earned a fan." As I looked at her with a confused expression on my face, she continued. "She expected this to be a fight and was taken aback at your approach. She admitted they might have gone to extremes, reading meaning into your message as well as responding based on working with others in the past on a similar project but was overly impressed with the current outcome."

Flash-forward a few years, I was promoted, and that systems team now reports to me! The goodwill I created in that one tiny instance came back in 100% support. If I had handled it in a way where I didn't try to see the other person's point of view, my future of being a leader of that team might have been in jeopardy and might not have gone as smoothly, causing issues not only for myself but for the company.

Owning your power by being adaptable and open to feedback does not mean you have to always take and implement the feedback given. When my director gave me the "intimidating" feedback, she knew if this feedback impacted my passion for driving the business forward, it would be a bad thing, so she gave the direction to take the feedback and apply it how I felt would be appropriate. And adapting my communication style to look for the intent and motivations of others served me well not only with that email message "mix-up," but in life outside of the office.

Be Patient and Stay Where You Are (Not!)

Before heading to a large corporation, I worked for a small non-for-profit where I learned so much that would impact me through the years. One of the best memories I had was when the vice president at the time was providing career advice. There was a job opening in the marketing department, and always eager to learn and move up, I wanted to apply. However, the vice president told me I was not a marketing person; she told me I was an operations person and that is where I would excel, so I should be patient and stay in operations. At the time, I was clueless. I had no idea what she was talking about with me "being" operations versus marketing. I clearly understand now that what she meant had everything to do with a difference in mentality and skillset—I have a tendency to lean towards an analytical and process mindset, which can strongly align to operations roles more than it aligns to a marketing role. However, at that time, I did not listen to her, and I applied and got the job! (No one else applied!)

If I am completely honest, though, I was not the best at marketing, and it was not something that came naturally or that I even really enjoyed. But I learned countless lessons that paved the way for future decisions, and for that and at that point in my career, it was worth going against the feedback. But it was feedback I still remember today. Once again, I chose not to take action that was directed by the feedback; had I done that, then I would have never applied for the marketing position. Instead, I chose to learn more about myself based on the feedback and make adaptations as needed.

Power Point

It can be worth it to go against the feedback.

A young lady who was making a drastic career change reached out to me for mentorship. She was moving away from what she went to college for and what she had spent the last several years of her career doing to go into a completely different field and follow what she felt would lead to what she was truly called to do in life. She listened to all the advice from others and the best practices, decided the best way to apply all the feedback from these resources, and adapted this feedback to help her achieve her goals. Her ability to be open to everything, and at the same time, have the discernment to apply what was effective to help her was a beautiful thing to watch. In the end, she owned her power and made the career change.

Power Takeaways

The key to the power of adaptability is to be open and make the final decision on how you will take the information and act accordingly.

- If your immediate response is to be defensive or dismissive, or do you do the opposite and just follow others advice and do not advocate for yourself.
- Take ownership of your actions and take initiative in finding ways to improve your personal interactions and communication style. Doing so puts you in control and on your way to owning your power.
- Apply the techniques and lessons in this chapter to check yourself.

Power Thinking and Journaling

- Is there a reason for your first response to be defensive or do you always just agree with others?
- Is the person communicating to you in a style that is different than your own?
- Are you understanding the person's point of reference?
- Is this person different than you? Are their customs, gestures, or understanding of the situation different than yours?
- How can you adapt in this situation?
- How can you continue to own your power of adaptability?

- What additional books, classes or courses can you take to help you improve in these areas?

_____

_____

_____

_____

_____

_____

_____

_____

_____

Books That Help You Own
Your Power of Adaptability

Surrounded by Idiots: The Four Types of Human Behavior and How to Effectively Communicate With Each in Business (and in Life) by Thomas Erikson

Show Up and Show Out: 52 Communication Habits to Make You Even More Unforgettable, 2e by Bridgett McGowen

How to Hit a Curveball: Confront and Overcome the Unexpected in Business by Scott R. Singer

Bonus Section: Your Superpower is Your Personal Brand

"… Your reputation is everything. You build your personal brand through everything you do, whether big actions or small decisions, and that brand will stay with you …."

—Janice Fields, American business executive, speaker, and women's career development advocate

Now that you have read this book, possibly journaled along the way to answer the questions, and had some hard conversations with yourself, how do you move forward with your True North, developing your personal brand? Having a personal brand is what will guide you and direct you.

When you google "personal brand" there are so many different concepts that pop up. Most of them teach you how to monetize your personal brand, which is great if that is what you want to do in life. However, what I am referring to is the two to three key words or concepts that when people think of you, you want those key words to immediately come to mind.

Here are some examples to start your in this exploration:

- Genuine
- Kind
- Confident
- Adaptable
- Knowledgeable
- Mature
- Ethical
- Strong
- Approachable
- Charismatic
- Inspiring

Take a business card size piece of paper and write your two to three key words on it—your brand. I have one that I created some time between 2003 and 2005; it has only two words listed—faith and kindness—and it is still my guiding post.

This brand serves as a constant reminder of what you want your life and your career to become and what you want it to project to others. If you focus on it, it will help guide your decisions, and it will hold you personally accountable. It will also help you determine whether the advice you seek while talking to others, reading content, or listening to podcasts applies to you or not—whether the advice will work to help you or if it will go against your personal brand.

For instance, there are some amazing experts and big names out there who are making millions and billions of dollars but with whom I personally do not align because their messaging does not align with my brand, and that is perfectly fine. We don't all have to agree; it's not agreeing that, in part, is what makes us uniquely different. It is beneficial that I understand their points of view, though, as it helps better educate me and keeps me grounded as to why I don't agree, and if asked, I can clearly articulate my dissenting points. But, if we do not know our personal brand and we try to take all feedback, advice, and knowledge and apply it, we might get confused and end up not finding our True North or having a muddled True North at best. And if you are unsure of where or how to get started, these books will provide some inspiration and direction:

Dare to Be Fabulous: Follow the Journeys of Daring Women on the Path to Finding Their True North by Johanna McCloy

I Am My Brand: How to Build Your Brand Without Apology by Kubi Springer

Personal Brand Clarity: Identify, Define, and Align to What You Want to Be Known For by Suzanne Tulien

In closing, I encourage you to review which lessons in each chapter of this book resonated with you and how they can help you identify and fulfill this personal brand. Maybe there are lessons you believe will work best and you can apply immediately, and there may be others that you will want to take some time to implement. If you there are too many and you feel overwhelmed, find the two or three that directly align with your brand; start there, then expand.

We cannot be great at everything, but there are some things that are truly natural to us. The other things we can work towards and begin to learn more about ourselves in the process.

When you own your power, you make an effort every day to achieve your full potential while impacting this world with even the smallest of actions. Your power is the strength of your thoughts, actions, and emotions. As you read through each chapter, truly dig deep and evaluate the Power Thinking questions as well as your journal responses to them.

Are you ready to take action? Are you done falling victim to the lies you tell yourself, your unconscious biases, and your limiting beliefs? Are you ready to place action before fear, to live to your full potential, and to continue to evolve and grow yourself? Was that a resounding "YES!"?

Congratulations on no longer giving away your power!

About the Author

Ginnette is a passionate problem-solver who excels at finding creative solutions to achieve exceptional results. Despite facing numerous challenges, including becoming pregnant at the age of seventeen while working and attending school full-time, Ginnette tackles each obstacle with determination and resilience. While her outspoken and Socratic approach initially led some higher executives to find her "too intimidating," Ginnette embraced their feedback and adapted while never losing her passion nor her ability to inspire excellence.

Ginnette's commitment to finding a better way propelled herself through graduate studies ultimately led to her become an adjunct professor in business, leadership management, and CAPSTONE classes for bachelor's and master's level programs. With more than twenty years of leadership experience, she has mentored countless individuals—from young adults to seasoned professionals—helping them unlock their full potential by owning their power.

Beyond her professional accomplishments, Ginnette takes pride in her role as a devoted wife and as the mother of two amazing children (and a dog)! In her free time, she can often be found hiking in the great outdoors, losing herself in a good book, or enjoying a cup of coffee.

www.ingramcontent.com/pod-product-compliance
Lightning Source LLC
Chambersburg PA
CBHW022103020426
42335CB00012B/806